India

Zaidee Lindsay

Adam & Charles Black · London

A & C Black (Publishers) Ltd 35 Bedford Row London WC1R 4JH

First published 1977
Reprinted 1983

ISBN 0 7136 1792 6

© A & C Black Ltd

Filmset in Ehrhardt and printed in great Britain by
BAS Printers Limited, Over Wallop, Hampshire

Contents

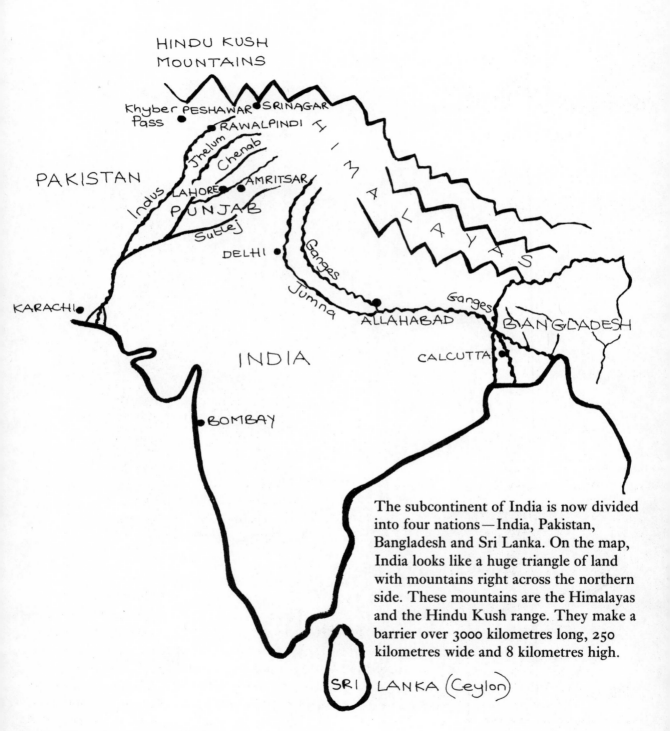

The subcontinent of India is now divided into four nations—India, Pakistan, Bangladesh and Sri Lanka. On the map, India looks like a huge triangle of land with mountains right across the northern side. These mountains are the Himalayas and the Hindu Kush range. They make a barrier over 3000 kilometres long, 250 kilometres wide and 8 kilometres high.

The subcontinent of India
(Ashish Dasgupta, age 14)

A war elephant,
carrying the barrel
of a cannon
(Imtiaz, age 13)

For centuries India's hot plains, river valleys, desert and jungle, could only be reached by climbing the mountain barrier from the north-west, using routes through passes carved out by rivers. The Khyber pass has always been the main route between Asia and India for traders and invaders alike. Over thousands of years, many races came to India. These peoples spoke many languages, and practised different religions. Strong religious traditions still decide much that happens in everyday life, and also divide the peoples of India even today.

The Hindus

Perhaps in no other religion have people brooded so deeply over the mysterious meaning of things. Hindus believe that Brahma, who is God, created the other gods and goddesses and then the earth, sun and sky. Hindus make pictures and statues of these gods and goddesses; some of them have animal form and many of them have extra arms, to show their great power. But each of these gods is just one face of Brahma. When a Hindu understands one of these faces, he is a step nearer to understanding the whole.

Ganesha, the Hindu god of good fortune
(Mehan, age 11)

6

Hindus believe that when people die, they are reborn into other lives — but whether they are reborn as a different animal or as a better human being depends on how well each person behaved in life.

At Allahabad, where the River Ganges joins the River Jumna, thousands of Hindus come each year to 'wash away their sins'. There are several holy rivers, and the Ganges is the most holy of all. Every pious Hindu hopes that, when he is dead, his ashes will be sprinkled on the Ganges at Benares, the holiest of cities.

Hindus try to make pilgrimages to holy shrines. The harder the journey, the more merit the pilgrim earns. Sometimes a horse is hired for the last stage of the journey.

The Ganges at Allahabad (Zia, age 12)

In northern India the *mandirs*, or Hindu temples, usually have pointed towers. A bell hangs over the entrance, and each visitor to the temple strikes the bell.

Pictures or sculptures on the building tell which god the temple is dedicated to. The white building shown here has its pillars and roof covered in decorative painting. Its gilded tower roofs can be reached by steps from the outside.

Some living creatures
(Sharda, age 12)

A Hindu temple or mandir
(Sharda, age 11)

'See no evil, hear no evil, speak no evil.'
(Ranjit, age 13)

These monkeys illustrate a saying popular throughout India, 'See no evil, hear no evil, speak no evil'.

The Buddha
(Soysa, age 12)

Buddhism

About 2500 years ago, a man called Siddharta Gautama taught a simple and kindly way of life: peaceful solutions could be found to all the problems of society, and people could stop seeking only worldly pleasure and personal success. Followers of Gautama gave him the title 'Buddha' which means Enlightened One. Today in India there are not very many Buddhists, but the noblest principles of Buddhism remain important in Indian thought.

Allah (Saleen, age 15)

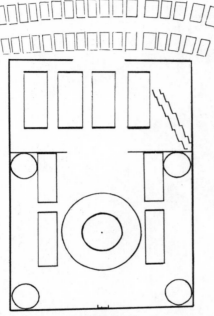

Plan of a masjid *(Nasim, age 13)*

A village masjid *(Khan, age 11)*

The Muslims

Islam—the religion of Muslims—is an important religion in the subcontinent, and especially in Pakistan.

Muslims believe that there is only one God, Allah, and that Mohammed is his last and greatest prophet. Mohammed lived in Arabia in the seventh century AD. Followers of Mohammed always discourage image-making, so pictures of Allah or of Mohammed are forbidden. Instead, children learn to write 'Allah' with extra symbols above: these are supposed to carry the sound of His name upwards.

The mosque or *masjid* may have a green dome and exterior adorned with gilt, or lavish decoration painted in colour. Both inside and outside, the decoration is only geometric designs, shapes made from stylised plant motifs, or texts from the Koran, the Muslim holy book. Muslims, like Hindus and Sikhs, respect their mosque by entering barefoot and covering their heads, and they also wash their hands, mouth and feet.

The masjid has two rooms, as you can see from the plan. One room has a domed roof, the other is open to the sky. Prayer mats are provided in the masjid.

Strictly, Muslims should offer prayer five times each day, but this can be done at home as well as in the masjid.

Traditionally a call for prayer was made from one of the minarets of the masjid, but now it is often done through a microphone inside, and relayed through loudspeakers on the roof. The devout then prostrate themselves in the direction of Mecca, the birthplace of Mohammed in Saudi Arabia.

New moon marking the beginning of Ramadan (Mohammed, age 11)

The Parsi Religion

The Parsis are descendants of the ancient Persians, who migrated to India when Arab Muslims conquered their country in the eighth century. They are one of the smaller religious sects in India, and are followers of Zarathustra, whose name is sometimes written Zoroaster. Fires burn on the altars of Parsi temples, while the dead are placed on 'towers of silence', left open to the skies, for vultures to devour.

In a Parsi temple, a sacred fire is kept burning. Worshippers bring pieces of sandalwood to feed the fire.

Sacred fire (Roy, age 13)

Vulture (Tariq, age 13)

The Gurdwara (Singh Brar, age 13)

The Sikhs

The Sikh religion was started by Guru Nanak about 500 years ago, in the Punjab area of India. Sikhs believe in one god, and have ideals of tolerance, equality before God, and support for the weak or oppressed. They had ten great leaders or gurus, and now they believe that their holy book, the Granth, is their guru for the present and for the future.

A Sikh temple is called a gurdwara. A village gurdwara, like a village masjid, is often a meeting place. People gather outside to watch a programme on the one television set in the village, or listen to the radio. Inside the gurdwara there are no seats. Everyone sits on the floor, to show that all are equal.

Festivals

Each religion has its festivals, which are part of their religious life.

Diwali is a festival of lights, held late in the autumn. The exact date changes according to the Hindu calendar—it is the Hindu New Year festival. Rows of lighted candles are placed along house walls and doorways. People exchange presents and send greeting cards, and shops are full of paper lanterns, toys and sweets. Diwali is celebrated by the Sikhs too, and they also celebrate the birthdays of their Gurus.

Dasehra is a ten day Hindu festival. Giant effigies of the demon Ravan are made and burnt and there are fireworks, rather like Guy Fawkes night. Charred pieces of the effigy taken from the embers are believed to bring good luck.

Dasehra (Mehan, age 11)

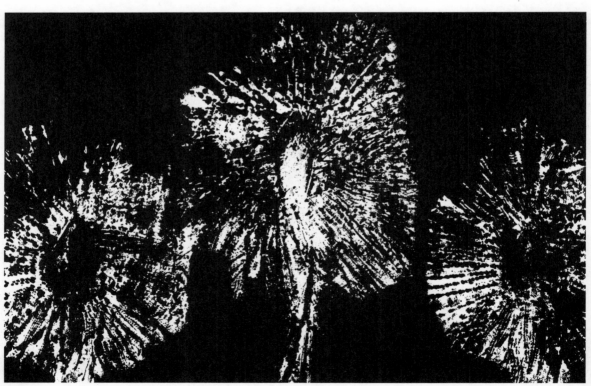

Diwali (Sunil, age 11)

16

The festival of lanterns
(Warusahennedige, age 11)

The date of the main Muslim festivals is fixed each year according to the phases of the moon. 'Big' or 'main' Eid is when Muslims remember how Abraham took the decision to kill his son as a test of obedience to God. Little Eid celebrates the Koran. It comes at the end of Ramadan, the month of fasting. Presents and cards are exchanged on both festivals.

In Sri Lanka there is a festival of lanterns in honour of the Buddha, remembering his birth, death and enlightenment. White tissue paper lanterns on bamboo frames are hung from trees in towns and villages.

The Temple of the Tooth in Kandy is a shrine which contains one of the Buddha's teeth. A casket containing the Holy Tooth is carried each year by one of the sacred elephants in procession round Kandy.

The Parahara elephant, carrying the casket which holds the sacred tooth
(Wijeratne, age 11)

Sari (Rajesh, age 14)

Sari worn over shalwar
(Surindar Singh Sangra, age 14)

Costumes

The traditional dress of Hindu women is the *sari*. It is made from a length of material about $5\frac{1}{2}$ metres long and about $1\frac{1}{2}$ metres wide. This is wrapped around the waist to make a skirt, then draped across the front of a blouse, or *choli*, and then over the left shoulder, where the end of the material may be either left hanging or cast over the head. Saris can be extremely beautiful and are sometimes made of embroidered silk, edged with bands of gold or silver thread.

Parsi women wear their sari over the right shoulder instead of the left, and some Muslims insist that sari material must be made from a silk and cotton mixture, and not from pure silk.

In India many women wear a printed cotton sari, worn with a chiffon scarf, white *shalwar* (baggy trousers) and sandals.

The traditional dress of Muslim women is a long tunic or *khameez* worn over shalwar, with a scarf, called a *dupatta*. The shalwar fit closely at the ankles.

Shisha is stitchery combined with fragments of mirror, and is a popular form of decoration on women's clothes.

Khameez worn over shalwar (Shabana, age 14)

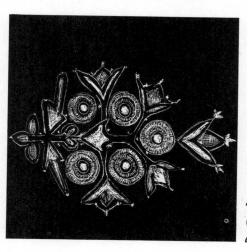

Shisha (Krishna, age 15)

The Pathan pattern (Akhtar, age 16)

The 'paisley' motif (Shakat, age 12)

One traditional Indian motif is known in Britain as 'Paisley pattern', named after the Scottish town where the motif was first imitated and printed on cloth. No one is sure what it represents, and many suggestions have been made in India—the mango, a palm flower, the cone of a flame, a bend in the River Jhelum or even the Ganges. In India the motif is long, but the motif is also found in Iran where it is more of an oval shape.

The Pathans of the North-West Frontier used to wear a distinctive pattern on the back and sleeve of their jackets, which has come to be known as the Pathan pattern. Their shoes too are known throughout India as Pathan style.

Even in the cities there are still many Muslim women who wear the veil. A girl may start wearing the veil when she is sixteen: the most popular colours are black and purple. All Muslims cover their head when reading the Koran, or listening to it being read.

The Jinnah cap is a *tarboosh*, named after the founder statesman of Pakistan.

Sikhs grow long beards and never cut their hair, but they keep it neatly covered beneath a turban. Sikh boys have their hair tied on top of their head with a white or coloured band or handkerchief.

A Pathan (Akhtar, age 16)

A Pathan shoe (Akhtar, age 16)

The veil
(Rashid, age 13)

Sikh boy wearing a
rumal, or band holding
his long hair in place
(Parnijit, age 11)

A Sikh turban
(Ranjit Singh, age 12)

A Jinnah cap
(Shaukat, age 12)

A Hindu bride (Rajesh, age 11)

A Muslim bride (Nahida, age 13)

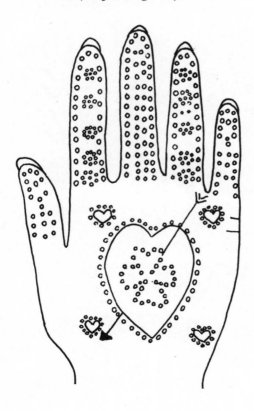

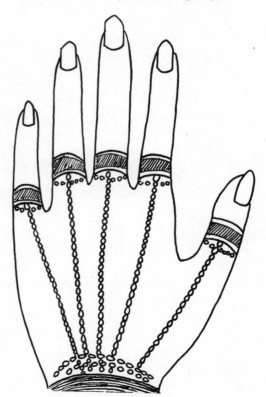

Hand decoration (Saleen, age 15)

The bridegroom fetching the bride (Sabri, age 14)

Marriages are sometimes still arranged by parents, and the couple have little or no choice. But this is changing and young people are now often allowed to choose who they will marry. Traditionally, a Muslim bride and her attendants wear ornaments on their hands, and their hands are painted with a greenish-brown paste called henna, which dries a bright orange colour and is hard to wash off. Red is the traditional colour throughout the subcontinent for the bride's dress and the bridegroom's turban.

Here is a Muslim bridegroom dressed in shiny clothes, perfumed turban, and with strings of flowers hanging over his face, fetching the bride to the ceremony on his flower-decked horse.

Snow in Kashmir (Bashir, age 11)

Land of Monsoons

The great rivers, the Indus and the Ganges, flow from the snow-clad peaks of the Himalayas. When the snow melts, and the heavy rains of the monsoon season pour down, all the rivers swell into rushing torrents, sometimes several kilometres wide.

Going to school in the monsoon season (Nachattar Singh, age 13)

Dams have been built to keep back some of this water for gradual release during the dry seasons of the year when drought is normal. The water is fed through irrigation channels.

In this picture Sikhs in the Punjab are fishing in a canal. 'Punjab' means 'five rivers'; the plains of the Punjab are the valleys of the Indus and its tributaries.

Fishermen (Nachattar Singh, age 13)

Bird in an irrigated field
(Nachattar Singh, age 13)

Carrying water (Krishna, age 15)

Usually the women carry water, and they wear a padded ring on their heads on which they can balance the water pot. During the dry season a villager may need to trek up to 15 kilometres to collect water in the pitchers slung on the donkey's back.

Donkeys, camels and buffalo are used to turn the wheels which lift water from the canals into the irrigation ditches, so that it can flow onto the parched fields. In June and July the Punjab plains can be hotter than anywhere else in India. Large white birds search for mice in the freshly irrigated fields of growing crops. A Sikh boy saw this bird in a field of sugar cane as he came home from school. Before the monsoon breaks, the weather becomes so unbearably hot that the ground burns your feet if you try to walk barefoot.

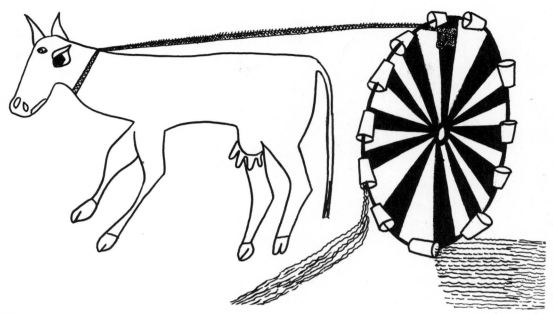

Buffalo working a water wheel (Akhbar Ali, age 14)

Boats and a raft on the River Jhelum in Pakistan (Ali, age 14)

Once the Mughal emperors used to travel with all their courtiers up steep, black, bare mountains, in order to escape the blinding heat of the plains and spend their summers in Kashmir, which was pleasantly warm. The ladies of the harem rode in golden howdahs on the back of elephants, the windows covered with gold mesh so that they could not be seen.

Elephants with howdahs (Saeead, age 11)

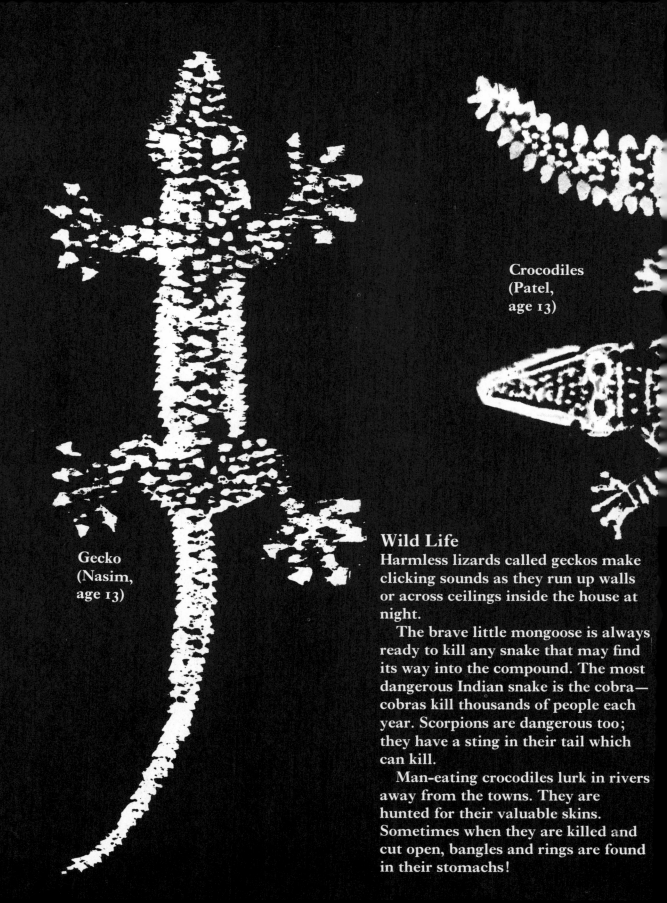

Crocodiles
(Patel,
age 13)

Gecko
(Nasim,
age 13)

Wild Life

Harmless lizards called geckos make clicking sounds as they run up walls or across ceilings inside the house at night.

The brave little mongoose is always ready to kill any snake that may find its way into the compound. The most dangerous Indian snake is the cobra—cobras kill thousands of people each year. Scorpions are dangerous too; they have a sting in their tail which can kill.

Man-eating crocodiles lurk in rivers away from the towns. They are hunted for their valuable skins. Sometimes when they are killed and cut open, bangles and rings are found in their stomachs!

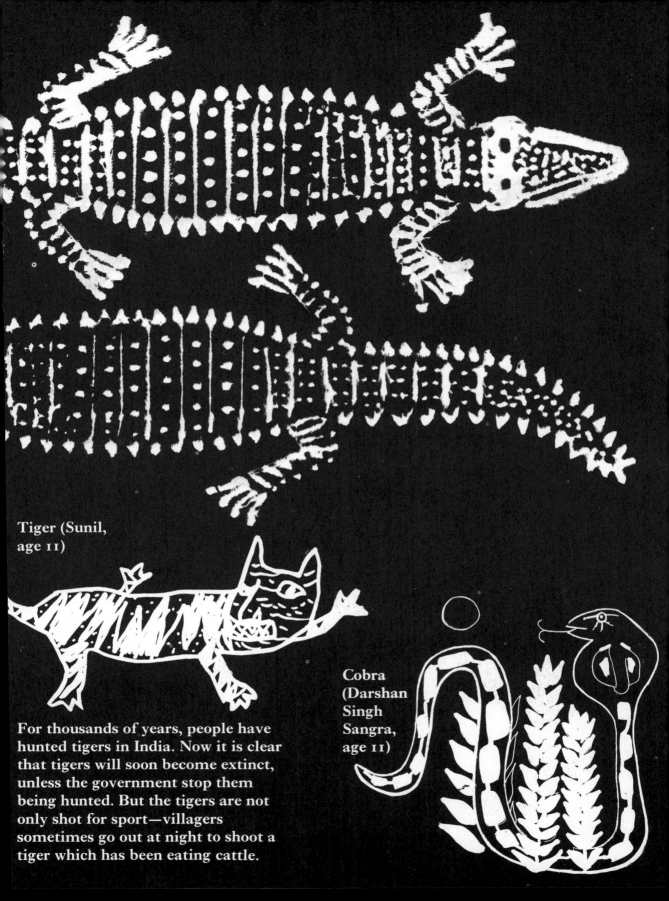

Tiger (Sunil, age 11)

Cobra (Darshan Singh Sangra, age 11)

For thousands of years, people have hunted tigers in India. Now it is clear that tigers will soon become extinct, unless the government stop them being hunted. But the tigers are not only shot for sport—villagers sometimes go out at night to shoot a tiger which has been eating cattle.

In some areas, monkeys live in the trees. The monkeys in the picture were swinging in a tree above a house; then they moved in a long line onto the flat roof, descended the staircase, and stole the chappatis which they could smell cooking below!

In Kashmir, as soon as the snow has melted enough for men and boys to walk without their bamboo snow shoes, they arm themselves with knives and axes and set out to hunt quails.

The grackle or mynah bird is a large starling. The largest species is the Indian hill mynah, which makes a talkative cage bird. It has glossy black feathers, yellow wattles, and a bright orange beak.

Peacock feathers are highly prized. They may be hung from the lamps of a masjid, used to mark a place in the Koran, or waved in bunches in a gurdwara. Muslim children are told that although the peacock is proud of its beauty, its feet are ugly: when it sees its feet, it is sad. This is a reminder that only Allah can be all-perfect.

A peacock motif for printing fabrics (Nusrat, age 13)

Monkeys (Narider, age 11)

*Elephants beside a road in Sri Lanka
(Warusahennedige, age 11)*

Quails in Kashmir (Mohammed, age 13)

*The grackle or mynah bird
(Shamas, age 15)*

A valley in Kashmir (Bashir, age 13)

A valley in Kashmir with houseboats moored among the weeping willows at the lakeside. There are apple, plum, cherry and almond trees in blossom in the distance.

Palm trees (Nusrat Ali, age 13)

Palm trees grow along parts of the sandy coast of the sub-continent.

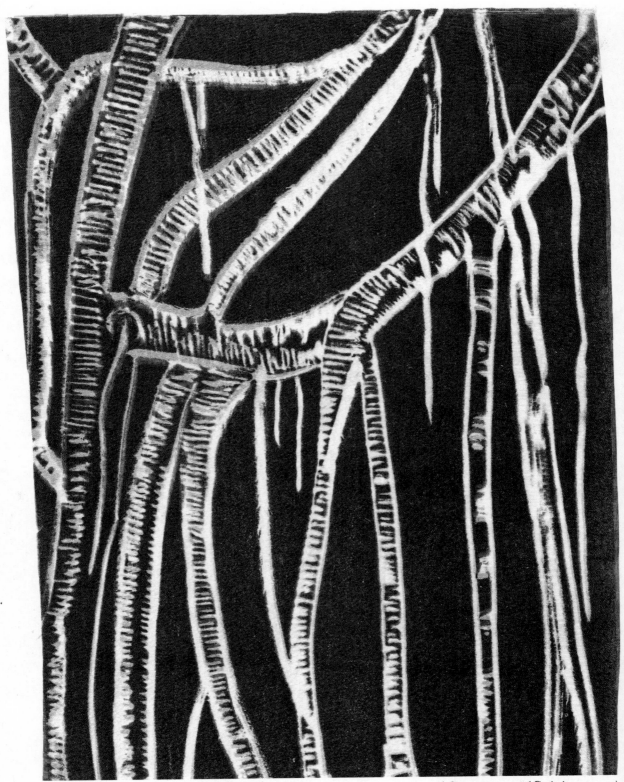

A banyan tree (Saini, age 14)

The banyan tree grows in India and in parts of Sri Lanka.

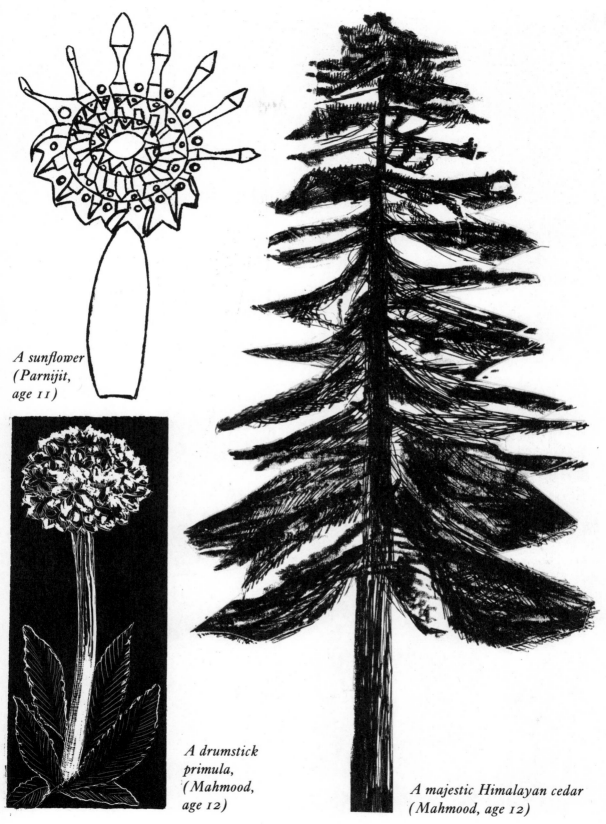

*A sunflower
(Parnijit,
age 11)*

*A drumstick
primula,
(Mahmood,
age 12)*

*A majestic Himalayan cedar
(Mahmood, age 12)*

The international port of Karachi (Farrukh, age 11)

Town houses in Pakistan (Nasim, age 14)

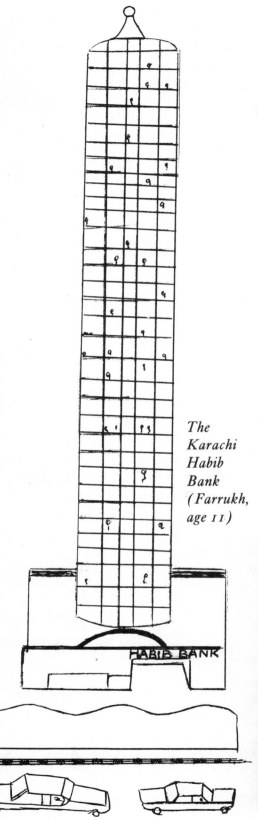

The Karachi Habib Bank (Farrukh, age 11)

Where people live

Although more people in the subcontinent live in villages than in towns, there are nevertheless large ports and modern cities.

In the cities there are terraces of white flat-roofed cement houses. There are alleys between the terraces, and the front door of each house opens from the alley into a small courtyard. Many of the houses have only a ground floor, with a ladder inside leading to a flat roof with low surrounding walls. In fact the roof is not quite flat, so that when the monsoon comes, the water can drain away. In Kashmir, where snow falls in winter, roofs are covered with straw.

In the villages, houses may be built in a compound, often next to the house of grandfather or uncle. Farming still depends on all the relatives sharing the work on each other's land. Inside the compound, farm animals are tethered near food troughs.

Our house (Sabri, age 14)

41

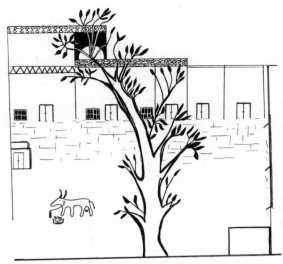

A village compound (Ali, age 13)

Some villagers like to paint patterns on their doors. Inside, the floors are sometimes made from flattened earth, or even from wet cow dung spread over the ground. This makes a flat surface, but it has to be renewed each week, as it cracks quickly. Sometimes the floors are made from concrete.

Beds or *charpoys* have short legs and wooden frames. Ropes are strung across the frame, and a bed-roll is laid over the ropes. On very hot nights some people keep cool by sleeping on plastic cloth, the end of which dangles in a tub of water. Many people carry their charpoy onto the roof or into the compound to sleep in the open air.

Design for painted door, Bangladesh (Ghafoor, age 11)

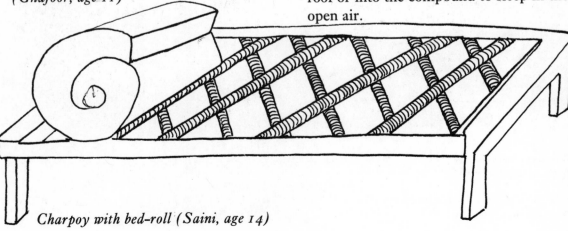

Charpoy with bed-roll (Saini, age 14)

A vegetable seller in the Bazaar (Chowdhary, age 13)

Occupations

For many millions of people, life goes on exactly as it has done for centuries. They are hardly ever in a hurry, giving the land an air of timelessness. The man selling vegetables in the bazaar, for example, is prepared to weigh out on his scales minute quantities of rice for customers.

A craftsman in Kashmir (Khan, age 14)

This craftsman in Kashmir is beating out metal oil lamps, even while he is sitting at his market stall.

A camel can carry a load of about 175 kilograms, so it is not surprising that in some Pakistani villages it is used to carry bricks for house-building. Camels or oxen are also used to pull simple ploughs.

44

A loaded camel (Ali, age 14)

A cow (Narinder, age 11)

Hindus allow cows to wander anywhere they please. They regard cows as sacred. This was originally because in a farming community cows were very important— the bulls were used to pull ploughs or carts, and there were never enough, so cows and their calves were highly valued.

A Sikh farmer using a bull to draw his plough (Surindar, age 12)

Water buffalo are used to provide milk. They have to be ridden out of the villages each day to their grazing places.

A taxi (Raja, age 14)

Some people still prefer to ride through the modern traffic in the cities on this kind of taxi. The name of the taxi-driver is written on the coloured canopy. Notice the shoes worn by the Muslim men: they are decorated with sequin patterns and flower designs.

Fishermen (Asanka, age 11)

Tree felling (Pal, age 11)

In some areas, elephants are used as bulldozers and tractors. They can use their foreheads to knock down trees, without hurting themselves. The men, who live in tents on the site, will then cut up the wood.

Jute plant (Patel, age 12)

The tall plant shown above contains a fibre called jute. It is cultivated on the Ganges delta near Calcutta. When the stems are three metres tall, they are cut, soaked in water and beaten. Then the tough fibres are left to dry. The jute is then exported to make canvas, sacking and cords.

This woman is picking leaves and shoots from tea bushes. Assam and Sri Lanka have become the world's most important producers of tea.

The rice crop is first sown by hand over a field. Then the field is flooded, because the plants grow best in shallow water. In the picture we can see the young plants being transplanted, three or four weeks later. They will still be underwater. There is a supply of plants laid out along the earth banks. When the leaves begin to turn yellow, the water is drained off so that the crop can ripen in the sun. Owing to the layers of rich silt brought down by the Indus and the Ganges, the soil of the plains of these two great rivers is so good that two or three crops can be raised each year.

Rice is the main food of the subcontinent, where most of the people are vegetarians. White rice is served with curries and vegetables, but it is sometimes coloured orange for sweet dishes.

Tea picking in Sri Lanka (Soysa, age 12)

Working in the paddy fields (Muthloob Hussain, age 14)

A firemaker (Arif, age 11)

A firemaker, who travels from village to village giving shows: he wears strange coloured clothes.

A snake charmer (Gurjant, age 11)

*Playing polo
(Ansar, age 11)*

Gulli danda (Tariq, age 13)

The hookah (Ahmad, age 12)

Musicians, with tambur and drum (Tauqeer, age 11)

This man claims he has found a dangerous snake near the village, and offers to take it away and kill it if the villagers pay him. He is a cheat—the snake is really a tame one which he takes from village to village.

Flying a kite (Mohammed, age 13)

Snake killer (Khalid, age 11)

53

Wrestlers (Ali, age 13)

The Maharaja (Sharda, age 11)

Indian princes have no power today, but some of them are still very rich. This one rode on an elephant through Chandigarh. He was wearing a large diamond on his blue turban and he threw money and necklaces to the crowd to make them happy. A man walked in front of the elephant, and musicians followed. The elephant's ears flapped up and down, fanning the air to cool it.

The illustrators and their techniques

Page	Illustrator, age & homeland	Technique
4	Ashish Dasgupta (14) Bombay	Felt tip
5	Imtiaz (13) Rawalpindi	Printed card, overprinted
6/7	Mehan (11) Delhi	Print from salt and cornflour
8	Zia (12) Allahabad	Pen and ink
8/9	Sharda (12) Punjab	Scraper board print
9	Sharda (11) India	Pen and ink
10	Ranjit (13) Britain	Impressed and cut on the surface of a cornflour an salt mixture; printed when dry
11	Soysa (12) Sri Lanka	Lino print
12	Saleen (15) Pakistan	Pen and ink
12	Nasim (13) Lahore	Pen and ink
12	Khan (11) Pakistan	Plaster print and pen drawing
13	Mohammed (11) Bangladesh	Plaster print
14	Roy (13) Bombay	Scraper board
14	Tariq (13) Pakistan	Lino print
15	Singh Brar (13) Punjab	Plaster print
16	Mehan (11) New Delhi	Plaster rubbing
16	Sunil (11) New Delhi	Scratched plastic
17	Warusahennedige (11) Sri Lanka	Screen print
17	Wijeratne (11) Sri Lanka	Impressed aluminium
18	Rajesh (14) New Delhi	Scraper board
18	Surindar Singh Sangra (14) Punjab	Scraper board
19	Shabana (14) Pakistan	Scraper board
19	Krishna (15) Bombay	Scraper board
20	Shakat (12) Pakistan	Pen and ink
20	Akhtar (16) Rawalpindi	Pen and ink
20 (two)	Akhtar (16) Rawalpindi	Plaster print
21	Rashid (13) Pakistan	Plaster print with net
21	Parnijit (11) Punjab	Pen and ink
21	Ranjit Singh (12) Punjab	Pen and ink
21	Shaukat (12) Pakistan	Pen and ink
22	Rajesh (11) New Delhi	Pen and ink
22	Nahida (13) Pakistan	Pen and ink
22	Saleen (15) Pakistan	Pen and ink
23	Sabri (14) Karachi	Impressed aluminium
24	Bashir (11) Kashmir	Lino print
25	Nachattar Singh (13) Punjab	Scraper board
26/27	Nachattar Singh (13) Punjab	Line drawing
28	Nachattar Singh (13) Punjab	Lino print
28	Krishna (15) Kathiawar	Pen and ink

29	Akhbar Ali (14) Karachi region	Felt pen
29	Ali (14) Pakistan	Scratched crayon on card
30/31	Saeead (11) Sialkot	Printed buckram, overprinted
32	Nasim (13) Pakistan	Impressed wood
33	Patel (13) Bombay	Polystyrene print
33	Sunil (11) New Delhi	Felt tip
33	Darshan Singh Sangra (11) Jandiala, Punjab	Felt tip
34	Narinder (11) Ludhiana	Scratched crayon on card
34	Nusrat (13) Pakistan	Impressed wood
35	Warusahennedige (11) Sri Lanka	Pen and ink
35	Mohammed (13) Kashmir	Plaster print
35	Shamas (15) Jhelum	Scraper board
36	Bashir (13) Kashmir	Scraper board
37	Nusrat Ali (13) Pakistan	Pen drawing
38	Saini (14) Punjab	Polystyrene print
39	Parnijit (11) Punjab	Pen and ink
39 (two)	Mahmood (12) Kashmir	Scraper board
40	Farrukh (11) Karachi	Pen and ink
40	Nasim (14) Karachi	Scratched crayon on card
41	Farrukh (11) Karachi	Pen and ink
41	Sabri (14) Karachi	Scratched crayon on card
42	Ghafoor (11) Bangladesh	Line drawing
42	Ali (13) Jhelum	Felt tip
42	Saini (14) Punjab	Felt tip
43	Chowdhary (13) Sialkot	Scraper board
44	Khan (14) Kashmir	Balsa wood print
44/45	Ali (14) Karachi region	Paper/fabric, printed and overprinted
45	Narinder (11) New Delhi	Felt tip
46	Surindar (12) Punjab	Plywood print
46	Raja (14) Karachi	Scraper board
47	Asanka (11) Sri Lanka	Scraper board
47	Pal (11) Sri Lanka	Scraper board
48	Patel (12) Calcutta	Pen and ink
48	Soysa (12) Sri Lanka	Scraper board
49	Muthloob Hussain (14) Karachi region	Scraper board
50	Arif (11) Bangladesh	Impressed aluminium
51	Gurjant (11) Punjab	Impressed copper
52	Ansar (11) Lahore	Felt tip
52	Tariq (13) Pakistan	Polystyrene print
52	Ahmad (12) Lahore	Polystyrene print
52/53	Tauqeer (11) Karachi	Lino print
53	Mohammed (13) Kashmir	Polystyrene print and pen
53	Khalid (11) Pakistan	Pen and ink
54	Ali (13) Pakistan	Impressed aluminium
55	Sharda (11) Chandigarh	Felt tip
End-paper	Ahmad (11) Pakistan	Cardboard print

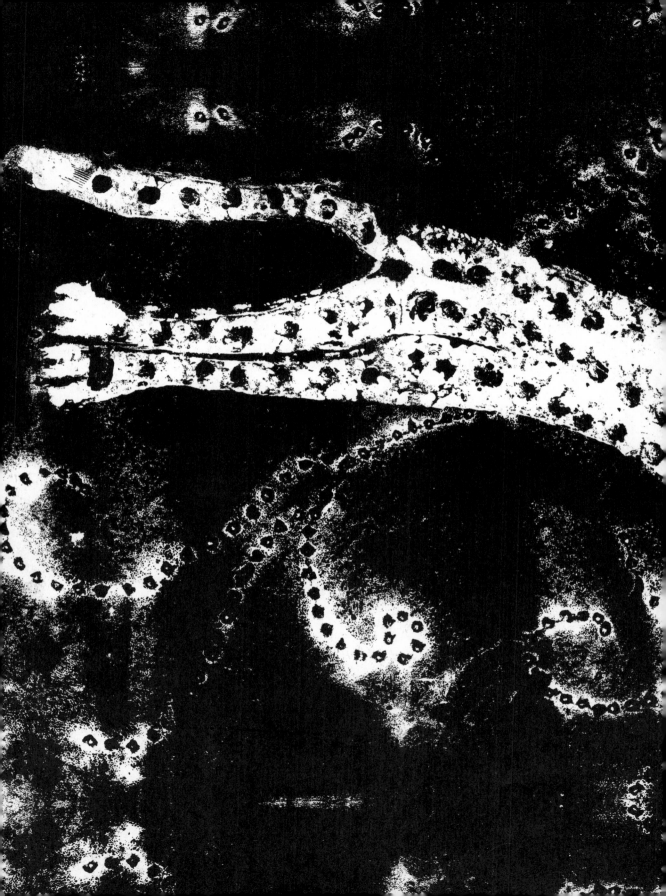